SILK TRAIL

絲綢
之路

Published by Nightwood Editions, P.O. Box 5432, Station A, Toronto, Ontario M5W 1N6 Canada.

Design by David Lee and Maureen Cochrane. Ideograms by Andrew Suknaski; other illustrations courtesy of the archives of the Vancouver Public Library. Typeset by David Lee. Printed in Canada by Gagne Printing. Published with the assistance of the Saskatchewan Arts Board; also with the assistance of the block grant programs of the Canada Council and the Ontario Arts Council.

Nightwood Editions is a division of blewointmentpress ltd.

Canadian Cataloguing in Publication Data

Suknaski, Andrew, 1942-
    Silk Trail

Poems

ISBN 0-88971-094-5

1. Chinese - Canada - History - 19th century - Poetry.
2. Railroads - Canada - History - 19th century - Poetry.
3. Silk - Poetry. I. Title.

PS8587.U55S54 1985   C811'.54   C86-093001-7
PR9199.3.S873S54 1985

with the assistance of the
Saskatchewan
Arts Board

SILK TRAIL

ANDREW SUKNASKI

NIGHTWOOD EDITIONS

to jimmie hoy & bill lee

SILK TRAIL

after "mulberry by path" anonymous /
ezra pound's cantos LII − XCII
and ma huan's ying-yai sheng-lan
/ the overall survey of the ocean's shores (1433 AD)

SILK TRAIL

from part III of *CELESTIAL MECHANICS*
/ life fragment in progress

a telling of how
           named things were
                      offered
      to tame terror
                 and pacify
                      the spirits . . .

sparrow hawk's cry
           bisecting
                 parallel worlds / /

           prairie / *ch'in*
                      rasp of
           pheasant . . .

cry merging
    dream
latitudes
  binding heaven
      to earth
       heart's
        geography /

nebo† / *nebiu* *
   the beyond
     some inner
   place . . .
heaven /

somewhere
  sun is always
   just
 pinching up
  over
 some wall's southeastern
    corner

---

†   Babylonian *god of wisdom* / Ukrainian for *Heaven*   *   Chinese political & celestial term

somewhere
        the long ranging
                soul
        is always
           a fabled
               incubus
        just colliding
            with someone's
        dream
          or doom . . .

somewhere
        there is always someone
                on horseback
      or on foot
          pondering dubious splendour
                  of betrayal
        and still dreaming
             a mere illusion
                  of someone else
        just as fair
           as lo-fu . . .

ming sha
   . . . ming
     sha
dreaming of
   sand
silk
  movements
     lo-fu's soft
flesh
  mostly spirit
     the way
a swallow's
   wing /
  cuts
   water . . .

2 trail of mulberry

> *a telling of they*
> > *who flee*
> > > *with child*
> > *in womb*
> > > *. . . the swallow's wing*
> > > > > *a brushstroke /*
> > > *naming you*
> > > > *god*
> > > > > *in water . . .*

> > *scant telling*
> > > *of surveyor*
> > > > *chao-kong*
> > *land*
> > > *kept*
> > > > *through hard work*
> > *land*
> > > *for keeping*
> > > > *silk-worm*

land
    clearings
          on margins of
    mulberry
        preserved . . .
    dream
      of silk
         ideogram
    merging
      happiness
         and truth . . .

somewhere
    luminous filament ————
         trail
  of mulberry ————

桑
樹

someone
  . . . *whose wife was it?*
  wang-ti's
          or an anon
          -ymous peasant woman
  be
  sure it was
  a woman
  5000 years
  back
        ——— *saw*
              the rare
                    possibility

of domestication
        less
            important
than
the glimpse
        beyond

. . . if we could
only weave it ————

    into something
    soft
        and light
        to wear

    we might walk
    nakedly
    as if
    we were always
    gently
        touched

by a mountain
wind
or
a swallow's
wing /
brushing
water . . .

a telling of ordinary things
as one
beneath nebiu / /

. . . ming sha
/ silk
trail
ming
sha . . .
faint
murmur
in a child's

 breath
  during
   sleep /

someone
  possessed
    by the worm's remorseless
  mandibles
      in
-gesting
      mulberry leaf becoming
           luminous filament /
  possessed
      as chao-kong
           . . . *wisdom of people is*
      synonymous
           with abundance
                of hill
           and stream . . .

somewhere
      someone

telling of things where

                 present moves

backwards

        in space

             doubling into future . . .

some tamper

         with nebo

             mystery

        outliving

           their God

some

    take time

        actually

    touch

      one

        another . . .

some

    talk their

        gift

into
 the dust . . .
    others
 talk one
   another
     to death
. . . the Word
    glimmering like
silkworm's
   mandibles
glutted /
 ——— *one*
 silkworm
 spins
 a thread
 one mile long ———

ju nujong sd
 "this filament
 this thread
 is your life ———

it breaks
or holds you
true
    to someone
    by pure
    intention ————"

a remembering of one
    treading
        water . . .

another
threading prairie time
        through the eye
of needling
    gravity ————

. . . *i don't wanna hear*
the truth anymore
jis wanna hear
    . . . *the sound*
    one footstep
    aheadda the other . . .

3 silk trail

    a telling of shaman

               binary time when

                             gods

               were still

                    heard

                        in parallel worlds . . .

               abundant

                    earth

                      the ordinary

             nature

                  of nourishment

                          and one's

                  healing . . .

    a telling of seeing

               the sea and soul's

                      true base

             co-ordinates

                  noted . . .

directions for crossing the ocean /
        note pei ch'en *star* (polaris)
        is 11 fingers
        high (17° 40′)
        and teng lung ku *stars*
        (the southern cross)
        4½ fingers
        high (7° 14′)
        this is your
        base /

micro-conversation

    old
        astro-physicist
        "it's right above you"

    youth
        "———— that's
        our northern cross?"

mountain
night
. . . the sound
one footstep
aheadda the other ————

one
dragging
eternity
as a ball
and
chain . . .

silk trail
. . . this is
your life ————
threading
through binary
dream /

. . . one pining
lost in

mulberry

forest

. . . another

musing

lost

among

pines . . .

revery /

. . . silk

weave it

right

a single filament ————

one

betrayal

buried forever

in the brain

———— *this is*

your life . . .

silk culture
           emperors
                in *ch'in*
    promising
           prompt death
                  to any fool
    revealing
           highly guarded
                secret

a simple telling
           of peasant women who
                    hide the sun's
           filaments
               / cocoons tucked
           under
             the hem

                  hsien
                      ——— portents of

tensile

terror . . .

eastern depot

during reign of

lung-ch'ing

gorged with

tight secrets

kept

by ample

gore and

exact

beatings

administered by

silk robe _____

guard

at meridian gate /

1587

year of the pig

final phase

of corruption

crumpling
     ming dynasty
having
   failed
     the common people

a telling of
  no time
    for breath
 or care

  "ming
   ——— *sha . . ."*

silk trail
  ——— who knows
     where
  it really
   begins?

  ma huan

              15th century
poet /
        interpreter
                    observed
in semudera

            "They have mulberry tree,
            keep silk worms.
            They do not know
            how to separate
            silk filaments."

further notes
              in *ku-li*
                      calicut

            "These people take silk
            of silk worm. Boil it
            till soft. Then dye it
            in every colour. They
            weave kerchiefs . . .

                    each one is sold
                    for 100 gold coins."

a telling of terms with
                    tartars
                            silk and silver
        keeping one
                silent
                        west of **WALL**
        transactions
                of heart
                        and desire ————

transactions
        silk trail ————
                            bandits
        and others
                moving along
                            drifting *ch'in*
                sand
                        ming sha . . .

from yinchuan
                    to western desert's
                                        jiayuguan
                    through gold
                            garlic
                            fears
religions including
                    uyguran mohammed
they of kashgar
            harder
                    to tame
        than the land
                ming sha . . .
silk road ⎯⎯⎯⎯⎯
                artery flowing with
                                everything
coalescing in
        dreams
                from silk
        linen
            jade

to performing dwarfs
and lithe
women
to spirited
horses
"sweating only
blood . . ."
the deep risk
of love
and
profit ————

silk trail ————
a filament
illuminating
the binary
dream
paralleling
worlds / /

sea
earth

flesh

ming
——— *sha . . .*

this is your
base /

silk
filament ———

silk dream . . .
of walking
as though
naked
or on
water
in dream . . .

floating entry /

rk
  "silk road
  ———— *God!*
i'd love
to travel across it
someday . . . "

silk dream . . .
            the risk
                    of prophet
              risk
              of shaman
                      and love ————

a dreaming of transaction
                  transgression
                              a game
                  of pure
                        chance
                                shuttling between
                  parallel
                      worlds / /

the dream
      of fortune
            the word
      that
         will
            change
———— *flesh*

        floating entry /
        dream
            the swallow's
                wing /
            cuts
              the heart . . .

"stick around handsome
you haven' even begun
to map me
or eternity . . . "
            murmurs
                ku ulyan

binary

muse

a divining for

the binary

dream / /

west / east

a taming

of the wild west

a taming

of the wild east

the taming

of flesh

an

expansion

into spirit —————

amour /

amur

river beyond
all rivers
where *ussuri line*
cuts
through
stone
into heart
of the wild
east /

ussuri line to
world line
cutting through
versions
of twin
paradox
/ interface
between
aging
and
the eternal ————

binary dream /

amour / amur ————

intimating love
            feeding
                    the spirit . . .
a telling of earth
                sustaining
                        the body . . .

        the world line
                    of love
        where
            time and
                    space
            merge
                with spirit
                        in naked
                singularity
                        of heart* ————

mohammedans
        levying heavy
              taxes

            the end
                of silk trail
                        ————— artery
                of love
                  and commerce
                        cut /
                in heart
                  of mystery . . .

dreaming of silk
        common peasants
              saw it
        as fleece on
            a shrub
              or tree
        sometimes
            thought
              imagined it

as fibre

      in inner

            bark ————

even hwui shan

      zen buddhist monk

                was deluded

      till two

            nestorian

                monks

      smuggled

            a handful

                of silkworm eggs

      out of

      ch'in ————

        floating revery /

        ———— . . . *damp*

        hollow

        willow canes

kept close
to heart
and body warmth . . .
———— *the flight*
to constantinople
522 AD . . .

the metaphysical irony
        that two
                nestorians
following constantinople's
            patriarch
should acquiesce
         before binary nature
                  of Christ
        as God and man
               mirroring one
        another . . .
and see their
        transgression
            woven into

byzantine
　　　　ecclesiastical
　　　　　　　vestments
of silk
　　　revolutionizing
　　　　　　　spirit
　　　binding east
　　　　　　to west ————

who knows
　　　who knows where
　　　　　　it all begins?

west / east

ming
　　　———— *sha . . .*

binary dream
    curving
       through
  latitudes
    of heart
  and
   celestial longitudes
  of
   desire . . . /

4 hwui shan

a telling of hwui shan
                    "star mountain"
                                  crossing 55° parallel
        west of
            TURTLE ISLAND
                        in 458 AD
        to meet
            autochthons
                further
                    down
           believing in
                magic
                  of jade
                      talismans
              and offerings
                    to gods . . .

hwui shan
        fascinated by
                coincidence

        . . . rites
            of passage
      jade
         stone
painted
       red /

placed
      in mouth
            of dead person
      before
        burial . . .

       floating revery /

       cranberries . . . in
            mouth
              of dead
             haida /

some autumn
          new bushes
berries . . . to pucker
          tongues
               of the
                    lil ones /

dream . . .
          of silk ————————
                    like the fabled
                              earwig
                    entering
                              skull . . .

dream . . .
          ch'in
               coolie yearnings
                         to move in latticed
               light
                    of GOLD MOUNTAIN /

a telling of anglo-search
for northwest passage
to the orient . . .

silk trail ————
ming
———— *sha* . . .
caravans becoming
too
slow
and
exorbitant . . .

star mountain
arriving
in new world /
GOLD MOUNTAIN
long before
and returning
499 AD
monk / missionary

                        drifting
NW
      in a junk /
                    the land
he named
                slowly
                    receding

      fu sang
            "many
                        voice
            wind"

      sifting . . . through
                        his lonely
      memories
                ———— filaments
                            of song

                    ———— *ming sha*
            ming
                    sha

———— *fu sang*
fu sang

rich
wind!
many
voice
wind!

burnished
teeth
gleaming
in
sun
an spray . . .

binary drift /
dream of silk ————
binding
heart
to faith . . .
dream

drifting
 . . . wind on ancient
                                        sail /
wind in
        some great tree
                        mountain
        named
            many
                    voice
            wind

bark's inner
                    fibre
stronger
        than silk

                ————— *fu sang*
the land
        silk
                would reach
someday . . .

54

in time
    a telling of silk movements
                where
  steamships enter
        sea swell
           trade winds
               ballooning
         clipper
          sails
  while
    engines are
        cut
  to accelerate
     the journey . . .

in hold
    the perfect
        ballast
    china tea
     and *bombyx*
          mori
    consuming
        bales of green
    mulberry
      leaves
        bound
      in hemp

a retelling
    this is your
    base /
     a vision ————
in hold
    ———— *heart*
      faith
   the perfect
     ballast ————

floating entry /

. . . *dear* elskan
hold me
      true to
      your sea

      where i sail
      or sink
      forever
      in your
      memory ————

o israfel
guardian spirit
illuminating
west ————

the illuminations
      of ancient lamas
            on GOLD MOUNTAIN

coin
ideo
gram /

      wherever this god
      of charms goes
              all evil spirits
              shall disappear

    doubt
        evaporating . . .

fu sang
      long known
           to *t'ien fei* /
      guardian
         spirit
            mirroring
      goddess
        of mercy ———— /

5 silk trains

THE GREAT

       ISLAND ——————

                TURTLE ISLAND

     "MANY
     VOICE
     WIND"

       . . . FU SANG

            VINELAND

NORTH AMERICA

GOLD
MTN!
     / collision chamber
             of the binary
   dream ————

            east is east
            west is
               west . . .

a telling of curved earth
                              and sea
                                   the way
mirages
          bend light
                    through space
          to erase
                    horizon ————————
                                   it was
                    an illusion
                              sometimes leading
                    mariners
                              from iceberg
                                        to iceberg

                    ———————— land
                                   glimpsed
                                        beyond
                    horizon ————————

entry /

eenuluapik

*"all same
        as westland"*

revery /

         northwest
            by land
    . . . *indeo*
         led them
  through
        waterways . . .

coolie dream
    . . . *GOLD MOUNTAIN!*
      wok
    thlee hunda
     dolla

go bok home
        CH'IN . . .

northwest passage

        a telling of search
                        and failure
        by sea
                and inland
                        waterways
        to *national*
                dream . . .
                        the consummation /

        glimmering of old
                        dream . . .
                                in a blur
        of memos . . .

        re CPR

        . . . as a consequence
        of the sparsely populated

character
of the country,
the supply of labour
of all kinds
is limited
and that having now
exhausted
their resources
of white labour
they have been
compelled
to resort to China
for men needed,
and have chartered
a number of steamers
for their
transport
          . . . interests
of the works
of the railway,
from the summit of
the Rocky Mountains
to the sea board . . . .

              Charles Tupper
              Min Railways & Canals

***

a telling of white
                   supremist
                             vision
                                   wadda ya say LordJesus boy!
                                   let's make the final push
                                   down through the mountains!

                   ***

TO HON SIR CHAS TUPPER

Prov govt are
enforcing
restriction law
& Coseq
steamship company
refuse China men passage
we need
men
to push work
please telegraph me here

66

immy
whether dominion govt
will interpose
           A Onderdonk

***

THE GREAT NORTH WESTERN COMPANY'S *MONTREAL*
AND DOMINION TELEGRAPH LINES

Jan 3 / 1880
                . . . it is beyond doubt
the the cost of the chief public roads
and other public works of the Province
has been materially lessened by the
employment of Chinese on these works
on which they were engaged year
after year working side by side
with white labourers without
disagreement or objection
by the latter until the recent
anti chinese agitation on the
Pacific coast extended into B.C. —————

... the Gov of B.C. sd ... 'the system
of Coolie[†] Labour defies
competition.'

Hon. Joseph W. Trutch

***

*   *

*

*   *

---

† "Coolie," one surfacing in the white supremist dream to work hard for little pay, etymonically grows out of *kūli*, the employed native labourer or servant in India and China. Other uncertain origins in etymon perhaps linked to *gulī* in Urdu and *kūlī* in Bengali. Perhaps identified with *kulī* and *kolī* of aboriginal tribe in Gujerat, India. Name likely conveyed to Portugese and on to South India and China.

a telling of dream

      . . . *the northwest*

               passage

                     consummated

in a line of steel

             ocean to

                 ocean

————— steel

          shining

              under moon

and northern

          cross /

         *   *

               *

         *   *

the train
slows
down
switches
      onto a
      sidetrack
      the prince
           walks out
           onto
           the observation
           platform
           holds his
           collar
           snug
           around his neck
           and turns
           from the
           arrowing snowflakes
           he demands
           an explanation
           for
           the delay

the conductor
proudly
replies

"sorry . . . your majesty
in this country
everyone waits
for the silk train
everyone
        it has rights
        over everything
        an God help
        anyone
                who doesn't
                wait ————"

HIGHBALL!
HIGHBALL!
HERE SHE COMES
HEADLIGHTS
DIMMING
THE LIGHT OF
THE STARS!   *   *   *

the conductor
looks
        at his
        pocket watch

 "good time
she left vancouver
three hours an forty minutes
after us
        an passed us
        an here
        it ain' even noon"

the silk train ———————
carries
more than
a million dollars worth
of silk bales
live silkworms
snug inside
each bale
——————— silkworms

feeding
on green
mulberry leaves
       the temperature
       perfect
       75° f
            give or
            take
            a degree
       humidity is
       nearly
        65%
            the fresh
            air
               is
               abundant . . .
       these
       conditions
       absolute
       -ly essential

a dispatcher
somewhere remembers

"they had a clear board
right across canada ————
there was never
a signal
     set against
     a silk train ————
     an God help
     the railroaders
     who let one
     be delayed . . ."

5 magic fading

dream ————————

        elusive

             and mercurial . . .

        brief

   lived

      glory /

        silk ribbons ————————

                neckties

            gowns

              sensuous

           -ly

             rustl

                -ing

             on

               the ball

           room

              floor

                  stalkings ————————

                       stockings

for debutantes
                    bright
-ly
    coloured
                    garters
    for
        follies ————————

        magic
                fading . . .

        mostly
                spirit
                        fading
                the way
                        a swallow's
                                    wing /
                                cuts
                            water . . .
                    ripples
                        smoothening

79

                                                like
                                            glass ————————

dream
    . . . silk ——————
                            something
        so
            perishable
                        only *lloyd's*
                                    of london
                        would
                            insure it ——————
    . . . imagine it ——————
                            beyond
                                    fact

        a single cocoon
                        yielding
                                400
                        to 800
                            yards
                                of filament ——————

imagine
           enough cocoons on
                              a single train
           enough
                 filament ————————
                                  to weave into
                 a thread ————————
                                encompassing
                                             the earth
                 . . . the world line

                                floating entry

                                ———————— *this is*
                                              your life

dream /
          the prince was
                      home
                          in time
                             for christmas . . .

dream
     innocence waning
               far beyond ussurii
    and
      amur ——————
           abandoned

                     while *white*
      express line
          boats
            empress of japan
empress of china
          and *empress*
              of india
        move
          spirited by
            trade winds
        with secret
           cargo
            chinese
        coolies

journeying with
                    tea
mail
      and raw
              silk ————————
  some coolies
          fortunate
                  enough
          to pay
              $500
          head
                  tax
  on arrival ————————

others
    shuttled on by
                white brokers
    those
        coolies
              travelling in
      bonded

cars with
        armed
guards
       in silk trains ————

floating dream /

      *   *

             *

     *   *

———— *beyond mountains*
                 the open
                     plain ————

    collision

chamber
of
   nightmares . . .

portents
                   ———— *the tensile*
terror /

this is your
base /
      debasing
                dream . . .

———— this is
                your life
your
      dream
                bound by
configur
             -ations
in

an alien
           land . . .

if you jump
           where
                 do you run
or hide
       in a barren
              land —————— *?*

how do stars
          or nebiu
                 keep one
        warm
             in winter . . . ?

they
      that last
          filament ——————
of magic
       fading
             in dream . . .

they destined
        for lives
of hard
    work
        in america
or west
    indian
        sugar plantations
where
    short ranging
        gouey
ghosts
    still
        search
for home
    on the margins
of local
    graveyards . . .

an intimating of
    "name

for name"
nebu /
　　nebo
amour /
　　amur

a telling of
　　binary
　　　muse **
　　ku ulyan /
　　　　elskan

　　　floating dream /

　　. . . ku ulyan

　　　mulberry ————

　　　PAIN
　　　TREE

松樹

> . . . elskan
>   pinned to
>   paintree . . .
> illuminating
>   east
> and west
>   on margins
>   between
>   parallel
>   worlds / /
> where
>   as swallow's
>   wing /
>   cuts
>   water
>   like
>   flesh . . . /

a relating of
      love
         "ming
               ———— sha . . ."
      they
        who vanish ————
                  like sand . . .
        sifting
            through
        ghost
           hands . . .

            floating entry /

             . . . ju nujong
                 softly
            murmuring
                  dreamer
            among
               ancients:

mountains melt
silk melts
we melt

time
. . . our
oldest friend
melds
seconds into centuries . . .

a scanning of
        the world line ——————
                            intersecting
        time
            and space
                    liquified
        into a mirror
                    or pool
        to glimpse
                ones
                    soul . . .

the interstellar line
        a circle
              where glaring
       Light
        the only absolute
                      . . . what you
        are
          in reflection
                 of what
        you will
            become . . .
      rules all
         co-ordinates
                 of heart
        earth
         and ordinary
                things ————

Home
> and Love
>> being
> the only
>> Queen
>>> and King . . .

floating revery /

——— *this is*
> *your dream . . .*
this filament
this thread
is your life ———
it breaks
or holds you

true
    to someone
    or something
    by pure
    intention ————

the price
      of arrival
          . . . whatever
you wish
    to call yourself
in these
    barrens ————

Acknowledgements

The author is grateful to John Newlove who edited this work. Many thanks to the Glenbow Archives and National Archives where some fragments of information were found. The author is also indebted to the Canada Council's support. Final thanks to David Lee's invaluable suggestions.

Bibliography

Huang, Ray, *1587: A Year of No Significance, The Ming Dynasty in Decline*, Yale University Press, New Haven and London, 1981.

Ma Huan, *Ying-yai Shen-lan: The Overall Survey of the Ocean's Shores [1433]*, translated and edited by J.V.G. Mills, Cambridge University Press for The Hakluyt Society, Cambridge, 1970.

Illustrations

All ideograms by Andrew Suknaski: page 17 "mulberry tree"; page 59 "many voice wind"; page 60 "gold mountain"; page 88 "pain tree." All photographs courtesy of the Vancouver Public Library:

Cover: Wooden bridge, Thompson River, 1899, CPR.

Page 2: Group of dignitaries cutting first sod for CNR, circa 1910.

Page 3: Great Northern Railway's Chinese track gang, circa 1909; location unknown.

Page 58: Roper watercolour of Burrard Inlet, Vancouver, West End in distance; date unknown.

Page 76: Chinese men aboard a CPR ship; date and location unknown.

Andrew Suknaski

"My deepest wish is to always retain a sense of place informed by innate duplexity where art emanates from my awareness that the greater possibilities and strength lie in dream time founded on a guilt vacillating between profound respect for the autochthons who first inhabited Turtle Island (or 'The Great Island,' as North America was first named) and my indigenous ethnicity predestined by a double code: the mythic mainsprings of a Slavic pantheism vis a vis the white Anglo-Saxon/Judeo-Christian cosmology. Believing my mythic origins and dream time to be twofold, I — through birthright — claim the inalienable right to honor both the aboriginal and white ethnic peoples who were mutually victimized by the white supremist. The obvious price of this art, built on the sentient wish to never fully empathize with a single people, is a guilt anchored in a deep sense of betrayal.

"As a Canadian writer, I am mostly concerned with finding a cipher that will decode a fourfold dream: the Anglo Saxon's dream and search for the Northwest Passage to further expand the British Empire (the human toll among many peoples being the price of that dream); the European immigrant's dream of a New Jerusalem in the new life (a second chance) in the New World; the Chinese dream of the 'Golden Mountains' in California, or the 'Gold Mountain' in Canada's West (the only chance for three hundred dollars and passage back home to be reunited with one's family and find another home elsewhere beyond crowded cities and states); and finally the Amerindian dreaming of homeland, *Manitou's abundance* to keep body and spirit where no boundaries are ever drawn — except by migration of game, and alluring mythical places where the gods impart their secrets."
(*Contemporary Authors, Volume 101*)

Andrew Suknaski was born in Wood Mountain, Saskatchewan in 1942. His most recent books include *In The Name Of Narid*, *The Land They Gave Away* and *Montage For An Interstellar Cry*.